I0117231

A Parent's Guide to the Special Education
Process from a Mom & Professional

NAVIGATE

and

ADVOCATE!

Tisha Eisenhuth, MSEd

NAVIGATE AND ADVOCATE!

A Parent's Guide to the Special Education Process from a Mom & Professional

All marketing and publishing rights guaranteed to and reserved by:

FUTURE HORIZONS

(817) 277-0727
www.fhautism.com

© 2025 Tisha Eisenhuth
All rights reserved.

No part of this product may be reproduced in any manner whatsoever without written permission of Future Horizons, Inc., except in the case of brief quotations embodied in reviews or unless noted within the book.

ISBN: 978-1-963367-41-6

Contents

FOREWORD

This book contains clear explanations of all the laws and programs for services that public schools should provide. Having this information in one easy to understand book will be extremely helpful for parents with special needs children.

In my own case, I had no speech until age four and all the symptoms of severe autism. When it was time for me to go to kindergarten in the 1950's, none of the regulations in this book existed. What made my elementary education most successful was when my mother and the teachers worked as a team. The rules at school were the same as the rules at home. If I had a temper tantrum, as it was called in the 1950's, I was not allowed to watch television for one night. But only one night as too long a punishment can be less effective. If I had a tantrum at school, the teacher would call home and tell my mother. It would not matter where my tantrum occurred, the consequences were the same.

Autistic children will often thrive when there is consistency between rules at home and school. Too often I have parents tell me that child may behave perfectly at home and have behavior problems at school. I have also had teachers tell me that a child that behaves well in school has behavior problems at home. In these situations, the parents and teachers need to work together.

NAVIGATE and ADVOCATE!

Both my mother and the teachers also worked hard to develop my areas of strength in art and building things. In the 1950's, all schools had lots of hands-on activities, such as art, sewing, crafts, and woodworking.

In an ideal world, all the regulations in this book would not be needed. The world is not ideal and it is important for parents to understand the laws that can help their child get the best education.

— Dr. Temple Grandin

Navigating Special Education as a Parent & Advocate

1

BE EMPOWERED

Being introduced to the world of special education can be intimidating. There are so many documents, so much information, so many acronyms, and so much jargon, and you find yourself sitting at the table with new faces who seem to speak a different language. I've been there, and I decided that in order to best help my child, I needed to select credible sources to read and learn all I could about my child's disability, the school process, the roles of members on school teams, and my rights as a parent. Little did I know this quest to support my own child would set me on a path to work in the field of special education, sit at the table as a professional to support other parents, and earn a Master of Science degree in special education. Regardless of their journey, I believe all parents and guardians have the ability to successfully collaborate and advocate for their children. Learning the main and plain components of special education can help make that possible. Research shows that strong collaboration between parents and schools leads to better student outcomes. Henderson and Mapp (2022) stated, "Successful partnerships between schools and families grow over time in a climate of mutual respect and consideration, maintaining a strong common focus on the well-being of the child." The key truly is *keeping the focus on a child* and what is in their best interest. Keeping high expectations while considering realistic ability levels is essential.

Imagine attending a special education meeting for your child at your local public school. You confidently walk into the room to discuss the Individualized Education Program (IEP). You have a folder of information about your child, including recent progress reports and a list of questions and concerns. You are ready to listen and speak with teachers, administrators, and any therapists attending. As the meeting opens, you already know the gist of what should be discussed and everyone's role at the table. You are prepared to ask questions about the documents and even suggest things to add or be changed. You aren't afraid to speak when opportunities arise and have knowledge of basic federal and state laws that may support any points of concern.

As a hypothetical example, let's assume you believe that your child should be included with non-disabled peers in school as much as possible. However, at this meeting, the principal states that your child must stay all day in a separate resource room because the school doesn't have enough staff and resources to assist your child in general education settings alongside "typical" students and that this would be best for everyone. You reply, "I hear what you're saying, but federal and state laws declare that every student has the right to learn in their Least Restrictive Environment. I don't believe spending an entire day in a separate setting achieves that. If my child can't do some academics in the general education setting due to needing small-group or 1:1 teaching, that's understandable. But I'd like the team to discuss what academic or extracurricular settings might successfully be attended with support, which may include classes like art, physical education, or music. You mentioned a lack of staffing … the law also states that financial or staffing challenges cannot be reasons to withhold services that a student needs. Denying my child the right to learn and participate alongside non-disabled peers isn't acceptable when research supports that students are more successful after graduation when they are included in the school and community with peers." You should then see the team discussion shift to brainstorming how and where more inclusion might successfully happen for your child. If that doesn't happen, then the special education director needs to be contacted to be part of the discussion, as the district should not want you to contact the state department of education for help because they are refusing to discuss your child's Least Restrictive Environment (LRE). Whatever the circumstances, speaking up and participating as a valuable member of the team can be you! As a parent, you have an equal voice on your child's IEP team. Be empowered to act respectfully but firmly on behalf of your child. The law supports your child's right to a Free Appropriate Public Education (FAPE). Let's dive in to learn more.

2
FEDERAL LAW

W hat is FAPE? This is a federal law that states must follow, but there is leeway concerning the types of educational programs schools may use. This law was originally created under Section 504 of the Rehabilitation Act of 1973 and entitles all persons with disabilities under the jurisdiction of a public school to a Free Appropriate Public Education (US Department of Education 1999). In a nutshell, this law protects children identified with disabilities from discrimination and holds schools that receive federal funding accountable to meet individual needs. Remember above when I mentioned inclusion with peers? FAPE states, "Students with disabilities and students without disabilities must be placed in the same setting, to the maximum extent appropriate to the education needs of the students with disabilities" (US Department of Education 1999). Schools understand that in order to provide FAPE, they are to follow the federal Individuals with Disabilities Education Act (IDEA) as well as their state laws. IDEA ensures special education and related services to those who qualify. It also discusses Least Restrictive Environment (LRE), which is ultimately the setting in which your child can best thrive. The US Department of Education (2004) states under IDEA that "special classes, separate schooling, or other removal of children with disabilities from the regular educational environment occurs only if the nature or severity of the disability is such that education in regular classes with the use of supplementary aids and services cannot be achieved satisfactorily" (Sec. 300.114). Here are examples of environments/programming from least restrictive to most restrictive:

- General education class
- Part general education/part pull-out for services, small-group or 1:1 instruction
- Special education classroom alongside children with similar needs
- Separate outside specialized educational facility
- Residential school
- Homebound or hospital instruction

It's a continuum in which a public school is to provide needed support in the broadest possible setting and only narrow down as determined necessary by a student's team. If needs cannot be adequately met in one setting, the school must look to provide access to another setting. The best setting will depend on what is best for a child according to their IEP, as one student's LRE may be quite different from another student's. Keep in mind that placement is not an "all or nothing" approach. A child may spend part of the day in a regular classroom and part of the day in a resource room (smaller group setting). For example, Billy may attend art alongside a full class of peers and then go to math in a resource room for the next period with six other students, where small-group learning and individual minutes of direct IEP instruction occur. See how IDEA can support the request for inclusion with peers under LRE? There are many ways in which public schools provide FAPE. This is just an example and the kind of information you can research online for yourself. The word "appropriate" in FAPE can be interpreted differently by different people, so that is something to be aware of that I will touch on later.

3
PUBLIC VS. PRIVATE EDUCATION

N ote that many parents choose to send their students to private schools. Please understand that unless a school agrees that it is unable to meet a child's needs (or it's been proven through data collection) and they pay for a student's attendance at a specialized school, then it is parental choice to unenroll a child from a public school to pursue an outside education. In my state of Ohio, this may include utilizing the Autism scholarship, Jon Pederson scholarship, or an EdChoice voucher, or opting to self-fund a private education. Important: When this happens, the right to FAPE has been waived or forfeited. This means that though the public school still bears the responsibility to evaluate and write educational plans for children who live in their jurisdiction, they are no longer required to carry out special education services and cannot speak to the quality of any outside services. The scholarship money could be used to piece together services from a state list of providers, or in finding a school on the list that accepts scholarship funds toward tuition. EdChoice vouchers are not disability based, may be accepted by certain private schools, and are basically scholarship amounts to help cover tuition. Unfortunately, at this time in Ohio, regardless of scholarship or voucher status, a private school is not held accountable for providing specialized services. No law requires that private schools be responsible for addressing the needs of students identified with special needs or implementing services listed in IEPs. In addition to not being required to provide FAPE, they do not fall under IDEA laws or have any of their services monitored or audited by the state. Private schools also do not have to follow state testing requirements, though some choose to do testing. They also don't have to admit or retain students like a public school does; they are permitted to choose to enroll or dismiss students at will. Therefore, though private settings turn out to be successful settings for some students, there are no legal state or federal protections afforded to ensure that they offer or carry out quality services a child may need, and the public school is not responsible for addressing any concerns with a private school on behalf of the parent or child. Different states may have different requirements, but even the US Department of Education (2011) stated "parentally placed children with disabilities do not have an individual entitlement to services they would receive if they were enrolled in a public school" (p. 2). I have often told parents considering private education that though some of these schools provide special services, be sure to investigate and trust who is educating and providing these services, since account-ability under the law is lacking. As you go forward reading, know that this guide is best designed to assist and address the process for those parents and guardians who have chosen public education as the path for their children. Services identified in an IEP must be provided by a public school free of charge to a family (other than things all families pay for, such as student fees). How are individual needs and services defined? Let's find out.

4

EVALUATION TEAM REPORT (ETR)

P art of providing FAPE is following a designated process under IDEA. "Child Find" is a term that means the public educational agency is responsible for identifying, locating, and evaluating students within their jurisdiction who have or may have disabilities. An Evaluation Team Report (ETR) is the blueprint needed to design an individual plan for a child identified with a disability. Some schools call it a Multi-Factored Evaluation (MFE). If you suspect your child has a disability (or has a medical diagnosis of a disability) and may require assistance, you can relay your concerns and request for assistance to your local school district, which would mean contacting the school psychologist in the building your child attends (or would attend). This can be done by email (considered a request in writing), and it's wise to copy a building administrator and even your child's teacher. Also include a summary of your main concerns. This would need to be tailored to fit your child. For example, it may be as simple as:

Dear Mr. Smith, Ms. Angelo, and Principal Stevens,

I am writing to request that the district perform an evaluation to see if my child, John Doe, needs special education services. I am specifically concerned about his continued struggles with content in academic classes, mainly math and language arts. I am also concerned about his speech and social skills, as well as his ability to use his hands/fingers for handwriting and other daily skills. John was recently diagnosed with autism by a physician, and I believe the disability may be having an adverse effect on his ability to learn in school. I am happy to provide that medical report as additional information to consider. I look forward to hearing from you and discussing the next steps.

Sincerely,

Jane Doe

Next, the school should schedule a meeting with you to discuss the next steps, as the school has thirty days to respond to your request. The school is also able to initiate this process by inviting you and a team of professionals to come together to consider an evaluation for your child. The members of this team include a school psychologist, an administrator, a teacher, a special education teacher, and maybe therapists, depending on concerns. The school psychologist is the leader of this process and will lead a discussion with the team at a planning meeting about what disability or disabilities the team may suspect. This will help decide which tests and screenings should be used. These might include assessments that look at IQ/cognitive ability, adaptive learning skills (the ability to do daily tasks, like dressing and eating), academic achievement and ability (such as for reading and math), and perhaps speech, occupational, or fine and gross motor skills. If behavior is a concern, a Functional Behavior Assessment (FBA) may be done to see what is triggering behaviors and if a Behavior Intervention Plan (BIP) is needed to encourage replacing negative behaviors with positive ones. ETR testing is done directly by the school psychologist, sometimes therapists, and additional observations and rating scales are often completed by teachers. Parents might also be asked to fill out rating scales about their child at home. If you are asked at some point to do this, try to be as honest as possible when filling these out. There may be the temptation to presume the best and score your child as performing higher in some skill areas than they actually are. Also remember that a child's behavior or abilities may look different in the home setting vs. the school setting due to different demands, expectations, and environments.

Sometimes parents aren't sure if the school did an evaluation after concerns arose, but their child may have received interventions available to all students. You would know if the school has performed or is going to begin a special education evaluation because parent/guardian consent (signature) is needed for ETR assessment to begin. Upon consent, the school team has up to sixty days to complete it. When finished, the school psychologist compiles all reports, and all areas are presented at an ETR results team meeting. The Ohio Department of Education and Workforce (DEW, 2022) created a

NAVIGATE and ADVOCATE!

helpful roadmap detailing this process: https://parentmentor.osu.edu/wp-content/uploads/2022/07/Evaluation-Roadmap.pdf.

Note that if the school does not suspect that a student might have a disability as defined under IDEA, they are able to deny performing an ETR at that time and must provide documentation detailing the decision (which should be kept if needed for future reference), called a Prior Written Notice (PR-01). If an ETR is compiled for your child, what should be clear from the results are the strengths and needs. What is your child good at? What areas are challenging? What support do they need in order to learn? Is a disability causing an *adverse effect* on learning at school? This information is presented as a lengthy document full of compiled data and can be explained in paragraphs, charts, and graphs. Don't let this intimidate you; the school psychologist and other team members can help you decipher these results. Your child's abilities will be compared to standardized scores of "typical" peers, meaning children of the same age who are not identified as having a disability. You will see averages and discuss where your child might be slightly below average, very below average, or even higher in some areas, as determined by the standardized scales. You may also see areas in specific tests that say things like "at risk" or "clinically significant." This can be daunting as a parent, as it can be overwhelming to look at several areas in which your child's abilities fall below average. Try to look at it as an opportunity to learn how best to help them move forward to be as successful as they can be. Getting support and school services is an important step.

To qualify for special education services, the data from the ETR must show that *specialized instruction* is needed, or that material needs to be changed and presented differently so that your child can learn content aligned with the general curriculum and make progress toward individual areas of need. Changes to the material to adapt lessons, tests, or homework are called *modifications*. A few examples include a third-grade student using spelling words that are at a first-grade level because the student currently needs this to help learn and make progress in spelling at his or her level. Or, a student needs lesson information presented differently, such as teaching them to use a visual organizer in language arts with altered content that only addresses half of the vocabulary terms for the unit. The goal would be to make individual progress and close grade-level gaps as much as possible. ETRs may also show that *accommodations* are needed so that a student can better access the curriculum. Accommodations don't change how content is presented, but may include things like sitting in the front of the room to reduce distractions, taking short breaks, a reduced amount of homework, and extended time on tests.

Please note: A student may need modifications and accommodations, but if the results show a student needs only accommodations, a 504 plan is most likely the appropriate option, as a student doesn't qualify for special education services if they do not require *specialized instruction*. In my experience, school guidance counselors collaborate with parents to write a 504 plan, but I have also heard of principals or assistant principals doing it. If the ETR data shows your child does not meet eligibility for special education services, ask the team about eligibility for a 504 or what other interventions within Multi-Tiered Systems of Support (MTSS) might be appropriate to help with the areas of concern. Many school districts have a tiered program in place.

NAVIGATE and ADVOCATE!

Upon reviewing this very first ETR, called the "Initial ETR," every member of the team participates in a discussion about the data compared to the potential disability categories discussed at the previous planning meeting when consent was signed. Important: In order to qualify for special education services, your child's needs must meet the definition of one of the fourteen disability categories under IDEA *based on the school setting* (if outside Ohio, check your state law concerning the applicable age range for the category Developmental Delay). These include:

- Autism
- Deaf-blindness
- Deafness
- Developmental delay (3–10 years)
- Emotional disturbance
- Hearing impairment
- Intellectual disability
- Multiple disabilities
- Orthopedic impairment
- Other health impairment
- Specific learning disability
- Speech or language impairment
- Traumatic brain injury
- Visual impairment

The team will need to review one or more of these definitions to see if your child meets the criteria. The school psychologist may read the definition(s) to you and share thoughts on how the compiled evaluation data does or does not support one of the disability categories the team agreed to screen for. Understand that only one category can be chosen in Ohio (some states allow more than one), and it does not have to "match" a medical diagnosis, but is based on the data from the school setting. That is a common area of misunderstanding that I have seen professionally. For example, a particular child may have a diagnosis of autism from a clinical psychiatrist, but when the school performs an evaluation, the data points to the category of emotional disturbance (ED). The family becomes upset that the school wants to choose this category (as emotional disturbance doesn't sound very good) instead of autism, but the school has no justification in doing that if their data doesn't best support that identification/educational definition. The school can provide you with these federal disability definitions, and they can be found online under IDEA. However, know that the point of the ETR is to identify your child's needs so they can be addressed in an IEP. Don't get too hung up over fighting about the category if the school is proposing to effectively meet your child's needs and help them make progress. If your child does not qualify under any of these categories after the evaluation, an explanation of why should be clearly written in a PR-01 along with any proposed suggestions concerning other supports, available school-wide interventions, or a 504 plan that may be appropriate at that time. If you really disagree with the outcome of the ETR meeting and are very uncomfortable with the results, you can request an Independent Educational Evaluation (IEE) at no cost to you, which means a qualified third party will perform an evaluation for your child. Keep in mind that this will subject your child to more evaluation, but sometimes it is beneficial, depending on the circumstances. Section 300.502 of IDEA states, "The parents of a child with a disability have the right under this part to obtain an independent educational evaluation of the child" (US Department of Education 2004). Procedural safeguards (guide to parent rights) addresses this, which I'll explain more about later.

Once the team discusses and agrees that the data does support that a student meets one of the above disability categories, each person in attendance signs that they participated in the meeting and checks that they are in agreement. If this is not made clear during a meeting, ask questions before you sign and agree! You should get a completed copy of this document with signatures at the end of the meeting or shortly after the meeting. The school must soon offer a date to reconvene for the IEP meeting so that everyone can look at availability. The school has thirty days to develop a draft of an IEP, and an intervention specialist should be reaching out to you. After a student qualifies for special education, the ETR must be updated every three years to redetermine eligibility (unless the team decides one should be completed a year or two sooner to screen for a suspected change in needs). I have told parents that at least a year needs to go by before the standardized assessments that were given can ethically be used again. The school is responsible for providing services up until age twenty-two (Ohio) if data supports this and the team agrees that a student should remain under school services longer than the typical graduation timeline.

Key Takeaways:
- If you are concerned that your child has a disability, request in writing that the school perform an ETR. (The school has thirty days to respond to you.)
- If current data does not cause the school to suspect a disability, an evaluation does not have to proceed at that time. The school may offer other options for support. (Interventions may be appropriate through district tiered supports or a 504 plan.)
- If the school also suspects a disability may be present, an assessment plan is agreed upon and the parent signs consent for the ETR to begin. (The school has sixty days to complete it.)
- The team will convene to discuss the results of the ETR and determine if a student qualifies for special education services under IDEA.
- If a child is found eligible, an IEP must be drafted within thirty days, and a case manager/intervention specialist is assigned to the student. (A team meeting is held to review the draft, edit, and finalize the IEP.)
- Data from a completed ETR may show that a student doesn't qualify for special education services at that time.
- Parents have the right to request an IEE if they strongly disagree with the outcome of an evaluation.
- A PR-01 should be issued after team meetings, describing the discussion and decisions, including details concerning any proposal or refusal to initiate or change the identification, evaluation, or placement of a student.

5

INDIVIDUALIZED EDUCATION PROGRAM (IEP)

An IEP is just how it sounds ... it's a plan designed to meet the individual needs of a child. You should not hear blanket statements like, "We don't do that here," or, "All students with autism learn in this room," or, "We don't have enough staffing to do that." As a child's needs are identified in an ETR, the team must discuss how the school will provide services that are appropriate to meet those specific needs. The word *appropriate* is important, because it does not mean the public school must provide the "Cadillac version" of everything, nor can it provide the bare minimum. Rather, the US Supreme Court (2017) ruled in the case of Endrew F. v. Douglas County School District Re-1 that an IEP must be reasonably calculated to enable a child to make progress *appropriate* in light of their circumstance. In other words, goals should be considerate of disability but be ambitious enough to provide more than a minimal or trivial educational benefit. In Endrew F.'s case, the school continued to provide basically the same IEP annually without the opportunity to meet challenging objectives. His parents refused to continue with an IEP that yielded minimal progress and pursued Due Process to ask the public school to pay tuition reimbursement after they withdrew and enrolled Endrew in a private school. The public school stated FAPE had been met because Endrew's IEP provided educational benefits "merely more than de minimis." Appeals eventually led to a Supreme Court ruling, which was important because it rejected the "de minimis" precedent and stated students deserve more than a minimal educational benefit under FAPE. IEP teams working to ensure present levels of performance are met with strong, measurable annual goals, and solid supports can help make this happen.

Another aspect to consider is expecting reasonable services and accommodations. For example, if your child needs additional support in classes such as math and language arts, the school might offer to write in the IEP that additional adult assistance is needed during class beyond the general education teacher in academic settings. This means an intervention specialist, or an instructional assistant (also called a paraprofessional) who works with the intervention specialist, will be in the room to assist your child and most likely a small number of other children throughout the period. The intervention specialist would also be responsible for any direct minutes of specialized instruction your student needs as identified in the IEP goals. If the ETR data does not show that a child needs adult 1:1 support throughout a school day and it's believed a student can make progress with broader support, then it is probably not reasonable to ask for an aide to be assigned only to your child unless there is strong evidence this is needed. Worrying about how a child will do when they transition from preschool to kindergarten or from elementary to middle school isn't a valid reason to ask for 1:1 support all day, even though it's understandable that parents may feel concerned about what is to come and how their child will adjust to major changes. As a team, we can't write services for what we anticipate *might happen* in the future, but must write based on what *is happening* now. If current plans continue to show poor results, then we can come back to the table to review data and discuss what adjustments may be needed. Keep in mind that data and team discussions drive decisions, and services agreed upon by the IEP team are to be carried out. For example, if the team determines that a child needs an augmentative and alternative communication (AAC) device to communicate (often called a "talker"), then that must be provided to the child for use while at school.

Important: If the plan the team agrees to put forth isn't working, parents or the school may call an IEP meeting at any time to discuss or make a change to the document, called an "amendment," outlining the new service or accommodation for just the area in question. The entire team does not have to redo a whole meeting and rewrite the entire document, as the relevant staff members involved with the change and an administrator can do an amendment with a parent. These are typically shorter meetings than an annual review of an IEP, and can be done in person, virtually, or by phone. The original review date of the IEP will remain, and the date the amendment was put in place will be documented near the beginning of the IEP. A PR-01 summarizing the conversation and decisions should always be issued by the school following a team meeting, including an amendment. An IEP can be a working document—it isn't set in stone for the year.

IEPs are divided and labeled into sections. In Ohio, the layout goes like this:

- *Future Planning* – This allows parents to share their vision for their child (areas of improvement, short-term or long-term goals).
- *Special Instructional Factors* – These are check boxes the team will discuss and mark depending on student needs.
- *Profile* – This may include areas such as student strengths, challenges, background information, medical information, recent testing results, daily functional skills, and progress monitoring.
- *Extended School Year* – These services are offered when data shows a student has shown regression after extended breaks from school or the team suspects it will take longer than appropriate to regain skills when a student returns to school. This is typically offered for a period of in the summer to students who qualify, such as three weeks, three days per week, for two to three hours per day.
- *Postsecondary Transition (ages 14+ in Ohio)* – Goals to help prepare for life after high school (addresses education or training, competitive employment, independent living). Checklists are answered by the student and/or parents on the student's Preferences, Needs, Interests, and Strengths (PINS).
- *Measurable Annual Goals* – Goals and objectives are defined, including skills the intervention specialist is responsible for

teaching and working on with a child. Specific progress is projected in a year's time. Includes Baseline Data/Present Levels of Performance (current academic and functional performance of a child) as well as a grade-level standard (statement of what typical peers are expected to be able to do at that grade level). Goals are numbered in this section (1, 2, 3, etc.).

Ohio State Support Team Region 11 (2022) provided instruction to school staff on what is required of an IEP goal (Section 6 of the IEP):

1. *Under what conditions?* – Describe the situation, setting, or given materials that need to be in place.
2. *Who?* – The child.
3. *Will do what?* – Observable behavior describing what the child will do to complete the goal/objective.
4. *To what level or degree?*
   a. How many times the behavior must be observed to consider the goal/objective mastered.
   b. The level of achievement required – avoid using unlimited cues/faded prompting.
5. *In what length of time?* – Timeframe to complete goal or objectives (no ranges).
6. *How will progress be measured?* – Select method(s) from the list on the IEP form. – The same method checked should be stated in the goal objectives.

For a closer look at this staff perspective on writing IEPs in legal compliance, view the Ohio SST11 (2022) professional

NAVIGATE and ADVOCATE!

development for staff tutorial: https://www.escco.org/Downloads/
IEP%20Basics%208882022.pdf

- *Specially Designed Instruction* – Includes services provided by an intervention specialist as well as related services like occupational therapy, speech therapy, physical therapy, or medical services that may be needed. Also included are any assistive technologies, accommodations, and modifications. Remember, accommodations help access content; modifications change how the content is presented (specialized instruction). The specially designed instruction section should include: Method of delivery, content, and methodology, as well as *who* is providing the instruction, *where* the services are being provided, and for *how long*.
- *Transportation* – Address individualized needs concerning school transportation.
- *Non-Academic and Extracurricular Activities* – Students with disabilities may have the opportunity to participate in activities just like their peers (needed support such as aide support may be discussed).
- *General Factors*
- *Least Restrictive Environment* – If a student requires instruction outside of the general education classroom with peers, a statement must be included to justify why the student must be removed to a smaller setting.
- *Statewide and District Testing* – Addresses types of tests a student will take and testing accommodations they qualify for.
- *Exemptions* – Excusal from testing consequences may be discussed and marked with justification.

- *Meeting Participants* – Attendance page to show who participated in the meeting.
- *Signatures* – This page addresses needed signatures, including agreement or partial agreement with the IEP. The very first, or Initial IEP, may not commence without parental consent and signature. Then services outlined in the IEP begin, and a copy must be provided to the parent within thirty days. A copy of Procedural Safeguards must be given to a parent/guardian at least once every school year (often offered with meetings).
- *Visual Impairment* – An additional section if needed.

Do note that a child's disability is not typically written on the IEP; it's more about addressing needs and building on strengths based on the ETR information. If it is important to you to have the diagnosis included, like autism or ADHD, then you may request that it be listed near the beginning of the document in the Profile/Section 3. Labels don't define a person, but you may be more comfortable having the diagnoses shared with school staff. You may also wish to share under "Other Information" (front page directly under your name and address) any medications your child takes or medical needs you'd like the staff to be aware of.

Unfortunately, I have seen mistakes made by professionals who write IEPs, particularly in Section 6 (Measurable Annual Goals) and Section 7 (Description of Specially Designed Services). We are all only human, but that is all the more reason for you as a parent to know how an IEP should be written so that you can make sure the documentation is solid to support your child into the next grade level or building. For example, if a teacher accidentally writes the services for goals in Section 7 out of order (not matching the goal numbers as outlined in Section 6), then the location and minutes of instruction may be listed incorrectly for the subjects. This might cause writing 80 minutes of instruction in a resource room for "Goal 1," thinking that is the language arts goal. But, "Goal 1" in Section 6 is listed as math, where the teacher intends to provide the student with 120 minutes of instruction in the resource room per month. This could cause confusion or a lack of providing services, especially if, for some reason, your child's teacher has emergency medical leave or your child switches school districts, as the IEP isn't well documented for another teacher to carry out. Bottom line: Learn the sections of the IEP and read through and make sure things are in order. The more eyes reviewing things, the better.

IDEA states that data on your child's progress (progress reports) should be given at least as often as report cards. Often, this means that a progress report will be sent home quarterly, or four times per year, with report cards. An exception may be if an IEP meeting is held within two weeks of report cards, as the current progress will all be covered then. Reviewing progress as well as attending parent-teacher conferences are great opportunities to see if your child is on track to meet their annual IEP goals.

6

IEP TEAM MEETING TIPS

A s a parent, the more you can learn what these IEP sections cover and why, the more you can speak on behalf of your child and ask questions. It's helpful to prepare a list of questions or concerns to take to the meeting, as it's easy to get caught up in conversation and forget things you wanted to address. Ideally, a parent should receive a draft from a few days to even a week before the IEP meeting in order to prepare to participate and note questions. I learned when my child was young to make a list to refer to during the meeting and highlight areas of the draft so I didn't forget anything I wanted to ask. If you don't receive an official meeting invitation, ask for it so you can see the list of everyone invited to attend. As the date draws closer and a draft is not shared because all sections aren't ready (such as waiting on a speech report), ask for a draft copy of the sections that are ready. Having the opportunity to read the Profile and other information ahead of the meeting can also save time during the actual meeting, therefore allowing more time to focus on goals and services. Remember that a draft is not a final plan, as you are to go through it as a team and make edits to finalize things. Then it can become a signed, legal document. In Ohio, all IEPs after the first IEP do not require the parents' signatures to begin to provide services, but the signature and check box are still wanted to show the agreement of the parents with the plan. There is also an option in Ohio to sign that you agree with all areas except for a specific area. Different states do this differently, as some areas of federal law give flexibility to the states on how to handle certain aspects of the process and documentation.

With all this being said, school staff participate in a lot of meetings. Sometimes it's easy for them to forget that all the terminology and information is personal and not routine to you. They may speak fast or move from section to section too quickly. If the pace of the meeting feels fast, ask them to please slow down (so you can process the information). Ideally, a staff member will ask if you have any questions after presenting a section. If they don't, you can politely interject and ask for clarification before everyone is off onto the next section and the opportunity is gone. Sometimes parents do not want to look as if they don't know anything or don't understand, which is totally understandable, but this hinders meaningful participation. When I first started attending special education meetings for my child, the team was helpful and kind, but it was overwhelming and I didn't completely understand my role in the process. (Should the professionals make the decisions while I listen, or should I be suggesting things?) Important: Engaged parents are experts on their children and will always have unique insights to offer. I also didn't understand the layout of the documents. I can remember reviewing the Initial ETR at home and becoming frustrated when I got a bunch of pages out of order. Allow yourself some grace in learning new territory but don't be afraid to speak up.

Keep in mind that if the IEP meeting has time constraints due to school or parent commitments, attendance (not agreement) can be signed to keep compliance with the due date of the meeting, and the team may reconvene another day in the near future to finish the discussion. This is better than rushing through. You also shouldn't see many staff members leaving very early or coming and going throughout the meeting, as your child's plan is important. If the edits the team discusses aren't made in front of you on a screen, you may ask for the opportunity to carefully read the final copy when it's ready before adding your signature (even overnight at home).

Furthermore, I would not recommend doing an ETR and IEP meeting back-to-back on the same day! ETR data drives the goals, and it's good to have time to digest the information before coming back to do the IEP. This helps prevent staff from rushing through the data or speaking too quickly, and also avoids teachers needing to leave early to return to their classes. It also prevents giving families the idea of "predetermination," or that the school decided ahead of time that a child was eligible to receive special education services (when it's a team decision). My opinion is that the information presented in one meeting is definitely enough for one day, let alone doing two meetings (unless it is a short ETR and a very simple IEP, with something like one goal and no related services/additional therapy).

NAVIGATE and ADVOCATE!

Not long after the IEP meeting, the PR-01 should be issued that summarizes the team discussion and decisions and addresses what is happening next (i.e., the annual IEP services are beginning). If you don't get this document and a copy of the IEP, make sure you ask so that you have your child's current plan and documentation about the meeting in case any questions or disputes arise about what was discussed (hopefully not). You will also want the final copy to monitor all the great progress your child makes. You might need to make additional copies of your IEP if you plan to apply for grants to cover outside therapy or to share with your child's physician or county board support specialist.

Another word of advice: Stick to advancing the meeting agenda and make sure to cover the most important information (goals and services) before you run out of time. To effectively advocate for your child, understand how you can best do it. Keep in mind that the main goal of the meeting is to set up your child for success. Prior events can sometimes cause emotions to resurface at a team meeting. Sometimes the air needs to be "cleared" or a parent wants to mention a concern that wasn't addressed before. However, take care to keep moving forward, as a divided team involving continual mistrust can be a recipe for disaster that won't help your child. Spending valuable meeting time on past hurts or misunderstandings probably won't help your child make progress right now. If things have been going well, that's great; continue to work together to support your child. Inevitably, there will be disagreements or bumps along the way. If you feel your school has failed your child in some aspect, try to address and resolve the issue as well as possible and move on with a positive attitude, as you don't want communication to break down or meetings to be continually filled with hard feelings and disagreements instead of discussing how everyone can help your child reach their potential. As parents, we can easily become emotional under stress, but you want to try to come across as being as *calm* and *credible* as possible. That doesn't mean you can't be straightforward and passionate. In order to best represent your child, be open to doing a little homework of your own. This may include reviewing your state's procedural safeguards and basic laws and considering what should be included in your child's plan. Keep in mind that parents are the only permanent members of IEP teams. Other members will come and go, but you as parents will be the ones to continue to collaborate and advocate as your child moves through the school years into adult life.

Important: Focus a lot on Section 6 in the IEP. Observe if the goals are SMART, which means *specific, measurable, attainable, results-oriented,* and *time-bound*. Are the goals clear so progress can be tracked? Do they seem ambitious, but like your child could meet them in a year? Do you know exactly what it looks like to master the goals? Do they state benchmarks during the year or by the end of the IEP? For example: "After reading a given leveled text, Billy will answer literal questions based on the text (Who? What? Where?) with 75% accuracy by the end of the IEP." Objectives or benchmarks would likely be listed under the main goal that address how he will build on skills to recognize the "Who? What? and Where?" in texts, and to track progress throughout the school year. Also pay particular attention to Section 7, the list of services. *Who* is doing *what* and for *how long*? Who is the professional providing the instruction? What are they providing? Where will it happen? Those are the types of things to really pay attention to and discuss. For Billy, this section could likely describe how the intervention specialist will spend twenty minutes per week working directly with him to identify those literal concepts using specific strategies, and that this teaching will happen in the resource room. If you have any questions concerning the teaching of the goal, the amount of minutes allotted for instruction, or the location in which this will happen, ask!

There is some flexibility on how goals are written, but also a compliant way to write them. Multiple areas of instruction shouldn't be lumped into one goal, but written as separate goals. For example, a math goal shouldn't include working on double-digit addition and working on telling time. The goals and objectives should be written as two separate math goals. Schools don't want to get dinged during an audit or have a family file a complaint only to find that an IEP was not written correctly. Pay attention to how your state IEP document is outlined; blank examples can often be found online under state Department of Education websites (the Resources in this guide has a link to Ohio's). Goals should always be based on high expectations, but keep them reasonable based on your child's current abilities. What's an ambitious goal that could be met by a year from now? Keep in mind that it may sometimes be better to prioritize and focus time on certain deficits first before moving on to more complex areas—you can't always cover *everything* needed in one IEP.

Important: Another aspect is being *available* to participate. Understanding and participating rely on your attention to the discussion and document and your willingness to be part of the team. Doing a virtual meeting while driving in the car, walking around the house with a baby, or doing chores isn't allowing you to do that. It's tough to hear of a situation such as a distracted parent agreeing to end a service in the IEP and then wondering later why their child isn't still receiving it. It can be difficult, especially for single parents, to make time for meetings around work and parenting responsibilities. However, work with the school to find a time that works for everyone. I would recommend in-person meetings with everyone sitting together around a table, as they're more personable and allows for face-to-face productive discussions. If a virtual meeting (i.e., Google Meet) is to happen, try to set aside at least an hour during a time when you can give the screen and your child's plan your undivided attention without interruptions.

As mentioned before, working together as a team is important. Hopefully, your child's school district creates a welcoming environment, but don't be totally surprised if you feel a little intimidated walking into a room and feeling outnumbered, like it's "me vs. them." That is typically not the intention of the school, but the environment can definitely make it feel that way. Taking someone with you can help, such as a spouse, friend, or relative who knows your child well; a parent mentor (if your school has one); or a specialist assigned to your family by the local Department of Developmental Disabilities if your child qualifies to be connected to county support. Proceed with caution if you are considering inviting a paid advocate, as this can sometimes create an adversarial environment and a tense relationship with the school. If you are interested in having an advocate attend, make sure they know a lot about your child and the goals and vision you have. Otherwise, I have heard accounts from fellow professionals and parents of advocates going rogue in meetings and fighting for things the parents didn't even want or that didn't improve their children's situations. That being said, that doesn't mean there isn't a place for disagreements or advocates, but remember, you want to do all you can on your end to maintain a positive relationship to promote the best possible outcomes for your child. It would also be polite to give the school district a heads-up if you are inviting someone to attend.

Also be aware that special education directors, principals, and superintendents have pressures of their own. They have to look at budgeting and where money comes from for services (federal, state, local). Some districts have more services available than others. Some have a full staff, and some are short-staffed (even after attempts to hire). States provide designated funding but also push school districts to fund much of their services through tax dollars. Some school districts pass school levies at the ballot box, and some don't. It is also a fact that the United States Congress has never fully funded special education as promised under IDEA in 1975. States are shorted millions of dollars each year for special education in the federal budget. I encourage parents to contact their representatives in Congress to advocate for the full amount of federal funding for special education as promised years ago. That all being said, when working with the school team, money is not for you as a parent to worry about when you address your child's needs. It's their job to figure out how to meet the identified needs and pay for services according to the law. Stay focused on what FAPE looks like, if the current school setting can provide for your child's needs, and how your child's plan will be carried out to meet those needs.

Also note that special educators face the challenge that some general education teachers they work with are not as knowledgeable in working with students who have thinking and learning differences, in carrying out IEPs, or in modifying material (but they share responsibility for the education of *all* their students). If your school district has several buildings and your child will be moving from one building to the next every few years and meeting new staff, it's a good idea to ask about an additional discussion or separate meeting before the end of the school year to discuss this transition to a new environment. I have experienced with my own child and as a parent mentor that though information is written in IEPs, having a chance to bring together staff members from two grades or buildings to discuss needed supports and schedules for the upcoming school year can save a lot of stress later. For example, you don't want to see your child get to a new building and realize a service looks different than you thought it would or find that your child isn't being sent to a class you thought they were going to attend. Try to make the path for the next school year as clear as possible with everyone on the same page (which also benefits children with challenges associated with autism or anxiety, since they thrive on structure and benefit greatly from knowing what to expect).

NAVIGATE and ADVOCATE!

Key Takeaways:
- IEPs are individualized.
- Learn the sections of the IEP and their purposes.
- Ask for a draft of the IEP before a meeting.
- Prepare questions ahead of meetings and ask when new ones arise.
- Have high but realistic expectations.
- Try to stay positive.
- Offer your perspective.
- Ask to make edits that help reflect a clear picture of your child.
- Understand how the school is going to address your child's needs (what, who, where).
- Be available to focus on discussing your child's needs—you are their voice.
- Don't continue to dwell on any past hurts—keep moving forward.
- Know what happens after the meeting (implementation of IEP, a follow-up meeting, etc.).
- Plan ahead for changes your student will face.

7

PROCEDURAL
SAFEGUARDS

S ince offering the Procedural Safeguards booklet to parents is an annual requirement, you may get tired of seeing it in paper or digital format. I, along with many parents who aren't strangers to special education, chuckle when we see it and say, "No thanks," when it's offered since we already have a copy (or several). However, it is important, as it states your rights as a parent and outlines the ETR and IEP processes. The right to request an IEE (mentioned earlier) is listed. Important: Often parents don't think of referring to this booklet, but then when a sticky situation arises (such as a disciplinary situation), the procedure is outlined in there. If a student exhibits behavior that defies rules outlined in the school policy and faces suspension or expulsion, there is a specific process that must be followed for students with disabilities, specific rules on how discipline can happen, and for how long. Understanding this process is essential if you find yourself in this situation, as it can already be an emotional time, and you need to know where to look. Also mentioned in Procedural Safeguards are FBAs and BIPs, and when they are required as part of behavior intervention and support.

Important: As well as addressing rights through the discipline procedure, Procedural Safeguards address the options involved in settling tough disputes between parents and school districts. (Read about "Facilitation" "Mediation" "Due Process.") I recommend, as much as possible, to do everything you can as a parent to avoid filing state complaints and creating continuous conflict. If you do contact the state, they will likely ask you what you have already tried in order to resolve the conflict. Don't get me wrong, a complaint has a valid place in some cases, when rights have been violated and the situation is not dealt with well or correctly. Procedural Safeguards also address educational records, outplacement to other facilities paid for by a school district, and notifying parents of the Autism or Jon Pederson scholarship opportunities in case they choose to consider private education instead of public. It is very helpful to read the Procedural Safeguards booklet if your family is new to special education, and it's important to review it periodically. Each state should have a version, but here is a look at Ohio's guide: https://education.ohio.gov/Topics/Special-Education/A-Guide-to-Parent-Rights-in-Special-Education.

Ohio also has a webpage dedicated to dispute resolution. Other states will have this process available to view as well: https://education.ohio.gov/Topics/Special-Education/Dispute-Resolution.

8

ORGANIZING DOCUMENTS

A suggestion for all of the documentation that comes your way: Keep the most recent IEP, progress reports, ETR, and state test results, as well as all BIPs, etc., organized in a three-ring binder. If there have been disagreements or disciplinary actions, you may also want to keep copies of your correspondence with the school. When your student finishes that school year or a few years in one building (i.e., middle school), you can remove these, put a rubber band or paper clip on them, and file them away. Another way to do this is to keep documents digitally on a computer flash drive. Keeping up-to-date with current information is helpful and may come in handy if your child encounters a difficult patch and you need to review progress toward goals, services, or other information. For example, if your child's teacher proposes to drop a goal and move onto something else since the goal of 75% progress was met, you might look to see if that percentage was acquired with heavy extra support or if it was your child's independent work. If your child is documented on a progress report to have only made 17% toward this goal while working independently, moving on to something more advanced may not be warranted yet. My point is, make sure you have easy access to your child's documents so you can back up your questions with facts. Sharing our feelings as parents is important, but feeling your child should be getting a service doesn't carry the same weight as showing the service should be given using actual data.

9
MEDICAL VS. EDUCATIONAL

Working with a private medical provider like a developmental pediatrician, clinical psychiatrist, or neuropsychiatrist can be very helpful. They can help with any needed medication management, and you can discuss with them concerns about home and school. Information from medical providers can be helpful to schools as well. However, there can be long wait lists (up to six to fourteen months) to see psychiatrists and developmental pediatricians who are qualified to determine a medical diagnosis. (No, a social worker typically cannot make a medical diagnosis recognized by insurance carriers.) Parents, beware that many places will advertise to give out quick diagnoses, such as for autism, even designating that label after a brief online consultation. If a disability is present, you want an accurate medical diagnosis and information to proceed on behalf of your child. Don't get taken advantage of.

NAVIGATE and ADVOCATE!

Important: Understand that your child's doctor may not "prescribe" an IEP that the school must draft. Sometimes, with waiting lists, primary care pediatricians are advising parents that their child's school needs to give them an IEP to get support rolling (when they should be advising them to reach out to the school to discuss concerns that their child may need an evaluation). Currently, the medical field has a habit of mentioning IEPs like this, which causes more confusion, because the entire ETR and IEP process detailed previously needs to happen before any services can. I have also heard of medical professionals telling parents that their children need intensive therapy, such as many hours of Applied Behavior Analysis (ABA) therapy per week. Parents are sometimes under the impression that the school will be able to provide all this therapy. When feeling pressured, some parents become frustrated and upset when the school is only following the law and can't just write an IEP or provide intensive therapy because of a doctor's note. Also know that different schools have different professionals on staff, or some contract out with companies to provide specific services to children who qualify, but providing multiple hours per week of direct 1:1 therapy, such as ABA, isn't necessarily part of providing FAPE. However, if a child needs something like direct behavior support, schools may consult with a board certified behavior analyst (BCBA) who specializes in ABA methods to help draft a behavior plan or to provide direct support. Remember, medical diagnoses and documentation from any outside counseling or therapy are always good information to share with the school in pursuing support, but they do not take the place of the special education eligibility process under IDEA or guarantee specific services in the school setting. I would love to see periodic state or county meetings between medical and school professionals to help address misunderstandings regarding their roles concerning treatment and education.

Another point to remember is that if you feel your child needs additional assistance, outside private therapy (such as speech, OT, PT, or even ABA) can be pursued by you as a family, and a set number of yearly visits are often covered by insurance policies. Speak with the pediatrician about referrals. You may find a service provider who can see your child outside of school hours weekly, monthly, or in the summer.

Some families are advised by physicians to choose many hours of therapy for their child instead of attending school. Remember that you as the parents (who know your child best) get to be the ultimate decision-makers, regardless of advice or pressure you feel from anyone. Weighing the severity of needs, suggested interventions, and opportunities to be around other children; considering financial aspects; and having time for your child to enjoy being part of the family and community are all things to consider when making these decisions. As someone who works in a public school and sends my child to one, I find it sad to see the scenario repeated of a physician pressuring parents to pull their young child from a public integrated preschool program to instead attend the hospital system's private clinical setting (including thirty to forty hours of ABA per week with an autism diagnosis) when the child is happy with their peers and making IEP progress academically and socially. I've heard parents wonder if they will need to quit their jobs (when they need the income) to try to facilitate getting their child to and from many hours of therapy. My husband and I were pressured by a physician when our child was four years old to do thirty-plus hours per week of ABA therapy. Our insurance did not cover it, initially sending me on a quest to look for various grant or scholarship opportunities to help (which still wouldn't pay for the cost of ABA). Besides researching the unaffordable hourly rates, speaking with other professionals who had worked with our child, as well as looking at the support and progress already happening through attending the integrated preschool program, helped us confirm the decision that our child would have a childhood and be included in school with same-age peers. We supplemented school services with additional outside therapies as time, using insurance coverage and paying some fees out-of-pocket. There are no regrets about this decision, but I recognize that all children and situations are different and plans should be individualized. There is no one-size-fits-everyone approach. Best advice: Consider all the information presented from doctors, therapists, and your school as *options*, not *orders*, and decide what is best for *your* child.

10
ROUTINE COMMUNICATION

C oncerning developing and maintaining a relationship with the school, keep in mind that just as you want to hear about the good things your child is doing right, teachers like to hear what they are doing right too. Something as simple as emailing a note, "Evan really enjoyed social studies class today. He has been talking about it all evening," or, "Thank you for the IEP meeting. We feel really good about the discussion and plan going forward." This encourages the two-way street of sharing information and working together. Something to keep in mind: If you ask to see work samples or have a specific question, a teacher may be caught in a week when they have four or five IEP meetings with all the documentation due. Try to give a day or two for a response, unless it is an emergency. Most teachers are good about trying to respond quickly. Using wording like "when you have a chance ..." can help show that you understand a teacher has other students to attend to besides your child. You can always send a gentle follow-up email if you don't hear back. I think you'll find a teacher may start sharing and reaching out to you more often when this type of relationship is established.

11

LONG-TERM SUCCESS AND HAPPINESS

Some parents get very concerned about their child staying at grade level and meeting all requirements of the general curriculum, which includes a lot of state and local testing. That's an understandable concern, but try to keep a mindset that the school, and you as the family, want to help your child do the best he or she *can* do. Learning and thinking differences can definitely throw up roadblocks, but keeping in mind the big picture is imperative. As a child grows and changes, academic work and social environments might also become more challenging. Behaviors may change along with biological changes, such as puberty. Years will pass quickly with different phases of life and education, be prepared that sometimes things may feel very smooth and other times it may be quite

NAVIGATE and ADVOCATE!

a bumpy ride. I once heard an intervention specialist say "There will be bumps in the road, but that's why we have seatbelts and airbags." I thought that was a good and supportive analogy to use. Furthermore, what we enjoy or think should happen in the future may not be what our children enjoy and think should happen. The steps they take after graduating must be something they are on board with in order to achieve successful outcomes. Transition assessments and services in the IEP help prepare for the future, and students are encouraged to participate in their own meetings in high school in order to have their thoughts heard (and we as a team need to listen). Looking into career centers or job readiness programs connected to your child's high school may be an option. Your child may also be eligible to continue to access school services past their senior year. Be sure to discuss these options as well as graduation requirements for your child. The Ohio Department of Education and Workforce (DEW) lays out these pathways to graduation: https://education. ohio.gov/Topics/Ohio-s-Graduation-Requirements/Contacts-and-Resources/Students-with-IEPs-and-Graduation.

DEW also provides a Roadmap to families on the topic of planning for the future and secondary transition: https://education.ohio.gov/getattachment/Topics/Special-Education/Families-of-Students-with-Disabilities/Sections/Secondary-Trasitions/Secondary-Transition-Roadmap.pdf.aspx?lang=en-US.

In 2021, Ohio had a graduation rate of 67% for students with disabilities (DEW 2023). The United States Department of Labor (2024) stated that in 2023, 22.5% of persons with a disability were employed. I'm not sharing these statistics as discouragement, but to encourage you not to wait until your child becomes an adult to start planning. Plans can be changed along the journey, but it's better to have a trajectory and something to aim for than to have a young adult sitting at home with nowhere to go. As your child approaches age eighteen, the school should make you aware that you lose guardianship, or legal rights. This means as an adult, your child becomes their own decision-maker and would need to invite you to participate in school meetings (as well as doctor appointments or to help with their bank account). There are options you may discuss as far as applying in your county/state for guardianship (most restrictive path) or supported decision making, such as power of attorney (can include just specific areas like education, financial, and medical) to support your child if they are unable to do certain things independently (collaborate with the school team, manage money, make medical decisions, etc.). There are law firms that specialize in special needs documentation and can answer specific questions. Ohio high schools can connect students with Opportunities for Ohioans with Disabilities (OOD) to help prepare for life after high school, including Pre-Employment Transition Services (Pre-ETS) beginning at age fourteen to explore career interests. Adults can also receive various forms of assistance through OOD: https://ood.ohio. gov/. There may also be job-readiness training programs, traditional universities, community colleges, or non-degree certificate tracks in your area that would be appropriate to look into.

All students don't have to eventually score high on state tests, SATs, or ACTs, or attend a traditional college or university to be successful in life. Happiness and success come in many forms. As your child grows and matures, homing in on their strengths and interests (and working on their challenges) will set them up for a future where they can play a meaningful role in life. Some students may head on to college. Others may do training to be ready to enter the workforce. Some may work full time, some may work part time, and some may enjoy volunteering often at an organization. Some may live very independently, and some may need additional support. Whatever the case, I believe that deep down everyone desires to be connected to something bigger, to be part of a community. After all, isn't it better for everyone, disability or no disability, to learn from each other at school and in the community? That can't happen if we are never together, so advocating for meaningful inclusion is essential. As parents who love and want the best for our children, it is imperative to maintain high expectations but also be realistic. One of my favorite quotes is "Keep your eyes on the stars and your feet on the ground" (Roosevelt, n.d.). Helping our children through school and life with this image in mind may be one of the greatest gifts we can give them.

12
ONWARD

n summary, I hope this guide is a solid resource for learning or reviewing the main components needed to successfully navigate the special education process as a parent, as well as offers new tips or insights into the professional perspective. The responsibility to help a child fulfill their potential doesn't fall just on home or the school—it falls on both! To be an effective advocate and voice for your child, remember:

- Learn basics of federal law (IDEA and FAPE) and be familiar with the requirements of the special education process.
- Know what should be included in ETRs and IEPs and their purposes.
- Speak up freely but respectfully as an expert on your child.
- Remember, decisions are to be made as a team.
- Organize and save documents. (Keep the most current handy.)
- Read and review the Procedural Safeguards (your rights).
- Be mentally and physically available to participate in meetings.

NAVIGATE and ADVOCATE!

- Maintain positive relationships with school staff and attend conferences.
- Identify and respect your child's preferences, interests, needs, and strengths.

And ... always have HOPE!

Turnbull et al. (2016) suggested the importance of parent-professional partnerships in promoting stronger outcomes for children with disabilities. Prepare and be empowered to navigate and advocate well, you won't regret it.

Disclaimer

Information on the internet is always changing, and you may find that some of the links in this book no longer work. Laws and processes also sometimes change. Do your best as a parent to research and look up current federal or state information as needed. Though this guide references many Ohio resources, there are many similarities in this information across states due to federal laws and guidelines in place.

Resources

Resources

Behavior Intervention Plan (BIP) – A plan designed by a child's educational and behavioral team to replace negative behaviors with positive behaviors.
https://education.ohio.gov/getattachment/Topics/Special-Education/Federal-and-State-Requirements/Ohio-Required-and-Optional-Forms-Updated/OP-2-Behavior-Intervention-Plan-Form-2024.pdf.aspx?lang=en-US

Blank Ohio Required and Optional Forms:
https://education.ohio.gov/Topics/Special-Education/Federal-and-State-Requirements/Ohio-Required-and-Optional-Forms-Updated

Blank Ohio PR-01:
https://education.ohio.gov/getattachment/Topics/Special-Education/Federal-and-State-Requirements/Ohio-Required-and-Optional-Forms-Updated/PR-01-Prior-Written-Notice-to-Parents-2024.pdf.aspx?lang=en-US

Disability Categories – Students must qualify under an IDEA category to receive special education services.
Ohio Disability Specific Resources Department of Education and Workforce (2023). https://education.ohio.gov/Topics/Special-Education/Students-with-Disabilities

Evaluation Team Report (ETR) – The ETR process is required under federal law by the Individuals with Disabilities Education Act (IDEA) and by state law, such as the Ohio Operating Standards for the Education of Children with Disabilities, in order to establish the presence of a qualifying disability, or disabilities, of a child suspected to have a need for special education services and supports from ages three through twenty-one years old. Ohio Department of Education (2024).

NAVIGATE and ADVOCATE!

Blank Ohio ETR Form:
> https://education.ohio.gov/getattachment/Topics/Special-Education/
> Federal-and-State-Requirements/Ohio-Required-and-Optional-
> Forms-Updated/PR-06-Evaluation-Team-Report-ETR-2024.pdf.
> aspx?lang=en-US

Free Appropriate Public Education (FAPE) – A free appropriate public education must be available to all children residing in the state between the ages of three and twenty-one, and it must be inclusive, including children with disabilities who have been suspended or expelled from school (United States Department of Education 2004).
> Section 300.101: https://sites.ed.gov/idea/regs/b/b/300.101

Functional Behavior Analysis (FBA) – The FBA is a structured data gathering process an IEP team uses to help identify positive behavior interventions and supports to be used in the school. An FBA is used to determine the answers to the following three main questions:
- Why does the student have challenging behavior?
- What reinforces the challenging behavior?
- What positive interventions help decrease the challenging behavior and increase the desired behavior?
  > *What is a Functional Behavioral Assessment, and how is it used? An overview for parents* (Pacer Center 2015): https://media.pacer.org/php/php-c215a.pdf

Independent Educational Evaluation (IEE) – The parents of a child with a disability have the right under this part to obtain an independent educational evaluation of the child. United States Department of Education (2004).
> Section 300.502: https://sites.ed.gov/idea/regs/b/e/300.502

Individualized Education Program (IEP) – Each educational agency shall adopt and implement written policies and procedures approved by the Ohio Department of Education, Office for Exceptional Children, that ensure an

individualized education program is developed and implemented for each child with a disability. Ohio Administrative Code (2002). Rule 3301-51-07 Individualized education program. (IEP).Ohio Administrative Code/3301/ Chapter 3301-51 | Education of Students with Special Needs.
https://codes.ohio.gov/ohio-administrative-code/rule-3301-51-07

Blank Ohio IEP Form:
https://education.ohio.gov/getattachment/Topics/Special-Education/ Federal-and-State-Requirements/Ohio-Required-and-Optional-Forms-Updated/PR-07-Individualized-Education-Program-IEP-2024.pdf. aspx?lang=en-US

Individuals with Disabilities Education Act (IDEA) – The Individuals with Disabilities Education Act (IDEA) is a law that makes available a free, appropriate public education to eligible children with disabilities throughout the nation and ensures special education and related services to those children. United States Department of Education (2004).
https://sites.ed.gov/idea/about-idea/#:~:text=The%20Individuals%20 with%20Disabilities%20Education,related%20services%20to%20 those%20children.

Ohio Department of Education and Workforce Dispute Resolution –
https://education.ohio.gov/Topics/Special-Education/Dispute-Resolution

Ohio Department of Education and Workforce ETR Roadmap –
https://parentmentor.osu.edu/wp-content/uploads/2022/07/Evaluation-Roadmap.pdf

Ohio Department of Education and Workforce Graduation Requirements for Students with Disabilities –
https://education.ohio.gov/Topics/Ohio-s-Graduation-Requirements/ Contacts-and-Resources/Students-with-IEPs-and-Graduation

NAVIGATE and ADVOCATE!

Opportunities for Ohioans with Disabilities (OOD) –
Vocational rehab and other services to support individuals with disabilities
pursue competitive employment opportunities.
> https://ood.ohio.gov/

Ohio Operating Standards and Guidance –
The Ohio Operating Standards for the Education of Children with Disabilities
(OAC 3301-51) are the state's requirements for providing special education
services to students aged three through twenty-one. They align with the federal
Individuals with Disabilities Education Act (IDEA) and outline specific
procedures for ensuring students with disabilities receive a Free Appropriate
Public Education (FAPE).
> https://education.ohio.gov/Topics/Special-Education/Federal-and-State-
> Requirements/Operational-Standards-and-Guidance

Ohio Procedural Safeguards –
A Guide to Parent Rights in Special Education. Ohio Department of
Education (2025).
> https://education.ohio.gov/Topics/Special-Education/A-Guide-to-
> Parent-Rights-in-Special-Education

Ohio Revised Code (ORC) –
Chapter 3323 | Education of Children with Disabilities.
> https://codes.ohio.gov/ohio-revised-code/chapter-3323

Prior Written Notice (PWN or PR-01) –
Prior written notice must be provided to parents a reasonable time before
the lead agency or provider proposes or refuses to initiate or change the
identification, evaluation, or placement. Prior written notice and procedural
safeguards notice.
> 303.421: https://sites.ed.gov/idea/regs/c/e/303.421

References

References

Henderson, Anne T., and Karen L. Mapp. *A New Wave of Evidence: The Impact of School, Family, and Community Connections on Student Achievement.* Austin, TX: Southwest Educational Development Laboratory, 2002.

Ohio Department of Education and Workforce. *Ohio's Special Education Determination – Graduation Rate.* Columbus, OH: Ohio Department of Education and Workforce, 2023. https://education.ohio.gov/Topics/Special-Education/Special-Education-Monitoring-System/State-Determinations#:~:text=Ohio's%2067%25%20graduation%20rate%20for,of%20all%20states%20and%20territories.

Roosevelt, Theodore. *As Quoted in Various Sources.* n.d.

Turnbull, Ann, H. Rutherford Turnbull, Michael L. Wehmeyer, and Karrie A. Shogren. *Exceptional Lives: Special Education in Today's Schools.* 8th ed. Boston: Pearson, 2016.

United States Department of Education. *Sec. 300.114 LRE Requirements. Individuals with Disabilities Education Act,* 2004. https://sites.ed.gov/idea/regs/b/b/300.114.

United States Department of Education. *Provisions Related to Children with Disabilities Enrolled by Their Parents in Private Schools,* 2011. https://www.ed.gov/sites/ed/files/2020/07/idea.pdf.

United States Department of Education. *Questions and Answers (Q&A) on US Supreme Court Case Decision Endrew F. v. Douglas County School District RE-1. Individuals with Disabilities Education Act,* 2017. https://sites.ed.gov/idea/questions-and-answers-qa-on-u-s-supreme-court-case-decision-endrew-f-v-douglas-county-school-district-re-1/.

United States Department of Labor. *Persons with Disability.* News release. Bureau of Labor Statistics, 2024. https://www.bls.gov/news.release/pdf/disabl.pdf.

Tisha Eisenhuth, MSEd, has navigated special education in a public school for thirteen years as a parent of a child with autism, and for eight years supporting other parents through the special education process as an Ohio Parent Mentor. Tisha's unique perspective has been shaped by these personal and professional experiences, and in collaborating with school personnel through both of these roles. This is what inspired her to earn a graduate degree in special education with a focus on autism. Her passion for helping other parents through the complexities of special education and supporting students of all abilities shines through in *Navigate and Advocate!* Tisha lives with her husband, Joe, and son, Zachary, near Cleveland, Ohio.

www.ingramcontent.com/pod-product-compliance
Lightning Source LLC
Jackson TN
JSHW062021291025
93191JS00009B/10